THE TOP 10 QUARTERBACKS OF ALL TIME

Cash Riley

A. Smith Media

CONTENTS

INTRODUCTION

Football has been a popular sport ever since its inception, though it is one that has been around even longer than that. In fact, the first two football games were played in England in the 1840s. Over time, many people have started playing football as a profession and many of those players are considered among the top 10 quarterbacks of all time. Over time, the rules of football have changed slightly but there are some things that continue to remain constant. Whether or not you're an expert or beginner when it comes to football and its rules, taking a look at these legendary players can be a fun thing to do whether you're watching a game or replaying through old highlights on YouTube.

Quarterback is arguably the most critical position in any football team. The quarterback needs to be able to throw accurately, read defenses, run the offense and lead his team to victory.

What does it take to become a great quarterback? We can answer this question. The top 10 quarterbacks of all time are known for what they did on the field and their ability to win clutch games. But these athletes demonstrate several qualities that transcend their achievements and make them more than just players.

Being a great quarterback is not easy. It takes many years of practice and dedication, but it also takes intelligence. Whether or not you like football, you need to know that intelligent leadership is always needed in every aspect of life.

Becoming a great quarterback requires a combination of athletic ability, outstanding football intelligence, and the right mental approach to the game. You need enough arm strength to make all of your required throws in the pass game, plus enough athleticism and mobility to avoid trouble when pressured in the pocket. The best quarterbacks are also quick thinkers who understand all aspects of offense and defense so they can quickly process information before making their decisions on the field.

If you want to play quarterback, it takes a lot more than the ability to throw and read defenses. You need to do your homework on all the little things that go into playing the game, from how to make a pre-snap adjustment to what steps you need to take after throwing an interception. This book will help you develop those skills and become a better quarterback at any level.

What makes a great quarterback? Some would say it's the ability to throw a perfect spiral, make the right decisions at the right time and have a strong arm. While these attributes can certainly help make a quarterback great, they aren't necessarily the definition of what makes an elite signal-caller. A passer's throwing accuracy alone is not enough; he must also be able to read a defense before the snap, make good decisions while under pressure during a game and lead his team as well as handle adversity with poise. Great quarterbacks also perform exceptionally well when it counts: in the fourth quarter or in clutch situations.

Here are my top ten best quarterbacks of all time.

OTTO GRAHAM

Otto Graham was a quarterback for the Cleveland Browns and the Brooklyn Dodgers. He's the only player to have won seven league championships. His nickname was "The Wizard of the Gridiron," and he was inducted into the Pro Football Hall of Fame in 1965. In 1964 Sports Illustrated named him as the greatest football player of all time.

Otto Graham played college football at Northwestern University, leading his team to three straight Big Ten Conference titles from 1940 to 1942 while winning each year's most valuable player award. He also led Northwestern to two Rose Bowls during this period (1941 and 1942). After leaving school early due to World War II service in 1943, Graham joined Buffalo Bills but never played a game due to military service obligations with Army Air Corps Reserve units near the Chicago area until 1946, when players were allowed back into NFL after the war ended; instead taking head coaching job instead with Western Reserve College (now Case Western Reserve University) where he first met future Browns owner Arthur "Mickey" McBride who hired former pro boxer Paul Brown as coach after firing previous coach Curly Lambeau because they were too old fashioned but knew how to make money even if they didn't win much which made them perfect partners

ROGER STAUBACH

In 1983, he joined the United States Navy and retired as a Captain in 1996. In 2001, Staubach was honored at halftime of a Cowboys game against the Philadelphia Eagles when his number 12 jersey was officially retired by the team. He also made an appearance at Super Bowl XLV, where he flipped the coin before kickoff.

Roger Staubach is the only man in NFL history to lead a team to the Super Bowl after taking over as a quarterback from the bench. Staubach should have won games and championships, but he was stuck with a mediocre Cowboys team for most of his career. Still, Staubach managed to win two Super Bowls and was selected for the Hall of Fame in 1985 with an 84% approval rate."

He is a quarterback and a Super Bowl MVP. He was an All-Pro six times and earned three Pro Bowl selections. He led the Dallas Cowboys to five Super Bowl victories, completing a record 155 out of 260 passes for 2,925 yards and 21 touchdowns in their victories over Miami and Pittsburgh in the 1970s

In 1985, Staubach was inducted into both college football's Hall of Fame and the Pro Football Hall of Fame (the first Dallas Cowboys to be so honored).

Staubach currently serves as president of JRS Enterprises LLC., a real estate development company based in Dallas, Texas. He also invests in companies like Citigroup Inc., Apple Inc., Bristol-Myers Squibb Co., Ford Motor Co., General Electric Co., McDonald's Corp., Microsoft Corpand Southwest Airlines Co..

AARON RODGERS

Aaron Rodgers is one of the most dominant quarterbacks in NFL history. He's a two-time NFL MVP; he led his team to the Super Bowl twice and has been named to the Pro Bowl on three occasions.

Aaron Rodgers is a quarterback for the Green Bay Packers and the reigning league MVP. He's an accomplished passer and one of the most accurate throws in NFL history. He has won two Super Bowls and been named to six Pro Bowl rosters during his career. He's also the current active leader in wins.

He's also one of the most accurate passers in history, completing 65% or more of his passes in six seasons (out of eight). His average season completion percentage is higher than any other quarterback, with at least 75 starts over that time frame.

Aaron Rodgers is the most-efficient passer in NFL history and has led his team to the playoffs in each of his 10 years as a starter, including an MVP season and a Super Bowl win. Rodger's passing efficiency is practically incomparable. He completes more than 74 percent of his passes, averages nearly 10 yards per attempt and throws more TDs (104) than interceptions (33) during games when he doesn't fumble.

Rodgers was also an effective runner out of the pocket early in his career – he had over 200 yards rushing and five touchdowns as a rookie before being forced to miss most of 2007 due to injury. But since then, he has not run for over 689 yards or tallied more than four touchdowns on the ground during any season.

JOHN ELWAY

John Elway is a quarterback who is still making headlines today. He was considered one of the greatest quarterbacks of all time and is remembered for many things. He was known for being an unstoppable force on the field, but he also had many accomplishments.

John Elway. The Broncos' famous QB has been a staple in the NFL for nearly 30 years now. Of course, playing for a team like Denver doesn't do much to hurt your legacy, but John Elway was one of the best quarterbacks to ever play football.

Elway played in more games than any other player in NFL history (303), making him an all-time leader in that category. He also won five Most Valuable Player awards and two Super Bowls with his team, the Denver Broncos—making him a legend on and off the field!

The most famous game John ever played was called "The Drive": It occurred during overtime against Cleveland Browns when John led his team downfield in 98 plays over 12 minutes before scoring a touchdown pass to win 35-20 at Mile High Stadium on November 28th, 1988.

DAN MARINO

Dan Marino is considered by many to be one of the best quarterbacks of all time. He played for the Miami Dolphins, winning two Super Bowls and making five Pro Bowls.

He holds many records in the NFL, including:

- Most Consecutive Games With a TD Pass (30)

- Most Passing Yards for a Season (6,084)

- Most Games with 400+ Passing Yards (6)

- Youngest Player Ever to Pass for 3,000

Dan Marino is the quarterback of our dreams. His cannon of an arm was the best ever and was just as accurate as the brains he possessed. He had a knack for making plays that were utterly outrageous once you saw them in person and could find his receivers with laser-like precision.

Dan Marino is one of the most celebrated players in football history. Considered by many to be the best pure passer in NFL history, he was named Most Valuable Player three times, led his team to four Super Bowls, and broke numerous passing records.

Dan Marino was one of the most prolific football players to ever play in a professional game. He set many passing records that still stand today, over 20 years after the fact. Dan Marino had

13 seasons with at least 3,000 yards passing, including seven consecutive seasons from 1984-1989.

Dan Marino is a football legend. He was one of the best quarterbacks in the history of the NFL and also performed well as an actor. Dan had a long career playing for the Miami Dolphins and his stats speak for themselves.

BRETT FAVRE

Brett Farve is one of the most talented quarterbacks to ever play in the NFL. His prolific arm strength and ability to improvise make him a dangerous quarterback. He is also known for his running abilities and has rushed for 12 touchdowns in his career.

- Played 20 years in the NFL

- Won 3 Super Bowls (back to back and then again)

- 2 time MVP

- Holds many passing records (TD/INT ratio, completions, etc.)

He was a gunslinger who didn't care about taking hits or throwing interceptions. He played with the Packers for 16 years and then went on to serve in the Navy for four years before returning to play for another five seasons. His TD/INT ratio is still one of the best recorded!

Records don't lie. Brett Favre is the all-time NFL leader in wins, completions, and passing yards. He also threw the most touchdown passes in league history, leaving Peyton Manning behind. In fact, he's been to the playoffs more times than any other quarterback in league history. If you're looking for a quarterback who can make every throw and lead your team to victory on any given Sunday, Favre is your guy. Brett Favre could throw the ball 70 yards without even looking at it.

PEYTON MANNING

Peyton Manning is widely considered one of the best quarterbacks in NFL history. He has won two Super Bowls, five MVP awards, and seven first-team All-Pro selections, among many other accolades. In his 18-year career, he has thrown for 71,940 yards (2nd all-time) and 539 touchdowns (1st). He also holds multiple NFL records, like most passing yards in a season (5,477 in 2013), and most seasons with 4,000+ passing yards (14). Most completions in a season (469 in 2004), most in an NFL career (7881), etc. The list goes on!

Manning was selected by Indianapolis Colts as the 1st overall pick during the 1998 draft after he played his college ball at Tennessee Volunteers, where he won the 1997 Heisman Trophy award given annually to college football's most outstanding player. Manning led Tennessee Vols to SEC Championship three times while setting numerous school records, including throwing 11 more touchdown passes than any other quarterback had ever thrown at Tennessee before him, which led him to win conference Player of The Year honors twice as well as being named All-SEC First Team selection four times and also second team choice once during those years when they were competing against teams like Alabama Crimson Tide who have some pretty good programs themselves down there.

JOHNNY UNITAS

Johnny Unitas was a quarterback for the Baltimore Colts. He played his entire career with the team, retiring in 1973 after winning four NFL championships and two Super Bowls. He was inducted into the Hall of Fame in 1979.

He is considered one of the greatest quarterbacks of all time and helped popularize passing as an offensive strategy. Joe Montana is another quarterback who won multiple Super Bowls during his 16-year career in the NFL, playing for three different teams (1979-1994).

Johnny Unitas, the original 'Horse', was the master of turning the game into a one-man show. He was an inspiration to others who followed him and his legacy has been consistently recognized by his peers and fans alike.

Johnny Unitas was the only quarterback to lead a team to three championships. He also was named NFL player of the year twice and won Most Valuable Player Awards in 1964 and 1967.

In the 1950s and 1960s, Johnny Unitas was considered the best quarterback in pro football. Unitas played his entire career with the Baltimore Colts, leading them to three NFL championships before retiring in 1974 as one of only six players in history to have their jersey retired by all-time team. He finished his career with a remarkable win-loss record of 128-27-7 in 17 seasons.

JOE MONTANA

Joe Montana is one of the greatest quarterbacks to play the game. He is a five-time Super Bowl champion, three-time Super Bowl MVP, two-time NFL MVP and Super Bowl Quarterback of the Year. Joe led the NFL in passer rating four times and was named First Team All-Pro six times in his career. Joe finished with 50,000+ passing yards and threw three touchdowns every game during his playoff career.

With exceptional accuracy, Joe Montana's quick release and deadly accurate passes set him apart from his peers. A five-time winner of the Super Bowl and three-time Super Bowl MVP, Montana could also tear up any defense on his own. His championship record speaks for itself.

Joe Montana was the face of the San Francisco 49ers franchise and was one of the most iconic NFL quarterbacks of all time. He led his team to four Super Bowl wins in the late '80s, cementing his legacy as one of the best players in NFL history.

Joe Montana is the greatest QB in NFL history. He had the innate ability to make plays with his arms and his feet. He could throw accurate passes on the run, and he was a magician at the line of scrimmage, manipulating defensive linemen and linebackers with subtle moves and skillful use of audibles. Don't forget, this guy came into the league with a bad back, so there you go—he was made of steel and willed himself to greatness on many occasions. He could have played in any era but rose to fame in 1980s San Francisco when he teamed up with Jerry Rice to form one of the best offenses ever

Montana was also one of the most athletic quarterbacks of his era and was regarded as one of the best roll out quarterbacks ever, often scrambling for positive yards in the face of pressure before taking shots downfield. Montana's career stats include throwing for 4,409 yards and 27 touchdowns among 20 interceptions during his postseason career along with a record 3 Super Bowl MVP awards. He also passed for over 3,000 yards during the regular season in 10 seasons.

TOM BRADY

Tom Brady is the oldest player to ever win a Super Bowl. At 39 years old, he became the oldest quarterback to win the Super Bowl, passing Brett Favre in 2010 when he won with the New England Patriots. This sustained success is largely due to his diet and lifestyle choices.

Brady takes care of his body by eating foods that are good for it and avoiding those that aren't. He follows a strict vegan diet during football season, which prevents him from having as many injuries because he's not putting stress on his joints while playing sports (no meat or dairy). The only time that he eats meat is when he goes home over the offseason and eats with his family; however, even then it's often fish or chicken rather than red meat like burgers or steak!

Tom Brady is the greatest quarterback of all time and has been since 2002. He's the best when it comes to team play, and his physical talent for throwing the football is not in question. His postseason record speaks for itself.

Tom Brady is one of the best quarterbacks of all time, and just so happens to be at the top of our list. Even though he isn't the most prolific passer in NFL history, he has shown a knack for winning — four Super Bowls, 50 game-winning drives, 172 TDs — and how important that can be.

Everybody loves Tom Brady. Not only has he been known as one of the best gamers in NFL history, but also as one of the most versatile. Yes, despite having less than Super Bowl titles compared to Peyton Manning, this amazing player has "won" more game-winning drives (4), passing touchdowns (172) and 50+ scoring games compared to Manning.

Tom Brady is the most accomplished quarterback in the history of football.

CONCLUSION

The best QBs are accomplished, intelligent and electrifying to watch. There have been hundreds of great quarterbacks, but these are a few of the best.

The NFL has seen a variety of talented quarterbacks throughout its history. These players are not just "quarterbacks", they are the players who created new standards in the game. They made their teams better, and they helped other players become even better.

AFTERWORD

I hope you enjoyed reading about the greatest quarterbacks of all time. These are just a few of my favorites, but there are plenty more to choose from. If you have any questions or comments, please leave a review!

ABOUT THE AUTHOR

Cash Riley

Cash Riley is a sports local columnist and author that specializes in ranking top players in all sports. He enjoys writing about athletes, both nationally and internationally, and bringing news, stats, stories and analytics to all readers.